The Busy Farmer

Matthew 13: Listen and Obey

CATHERINE MACKENZIE
Illustrated by Chiara Bertelli

CF4•K
Learn it: God is good
Do it: Listen to what God says
Find it: Who listens to you? Psalm 66:19

Have you ever planted seeds and watched them grow? What do you have to do in order to make sure your plants are healthy?

You need to water them and care for them. Make sure they have sunlight and shelter, so that one day, in the future, little flowers will appear.

Jesus once told a story about a field and a very busy farmer. However, Jesus wasn't on the land when he told this story — he was on the beach. People had gathered there. They wanted to hear what Jesus had to say. Jesus was going to tell a story with a special meaning. He wanted the people to learn more about God and what it means to follow him.

WHAT IS A PARABLE? A parable is a story that teaches you important truths about God. Jesus told these stories because he wanted people to understand that they needed to trust and follow God. Sometimes the people listened and understood. Sometimes they didn't. Sometimes they just didn't want to follow God at all.

A farmer went out to sow and as he threw the seeds onto the soil, some fell on the road and birds came and ate them up.

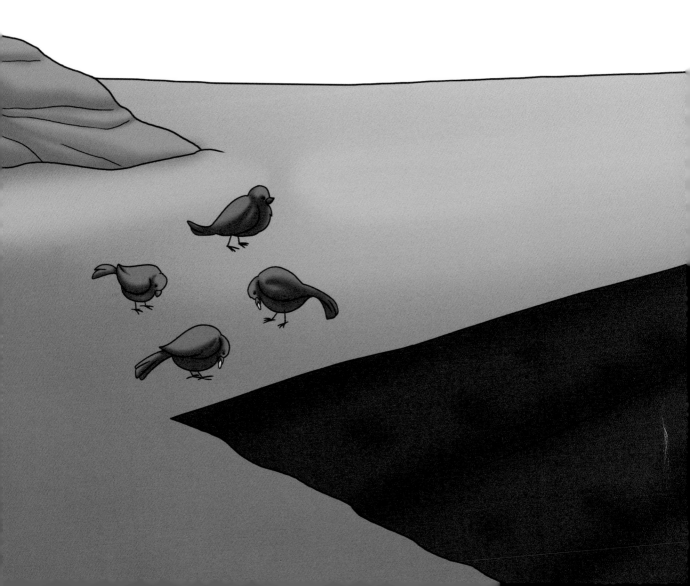

Some seeds fell on poor soil and so didn't have a chance to grow.

Other seeds fell on the rocky places. As soon as the little plants sprung up, they withered because of the hot sun. In the shallow soil their roots could not grow and the plants died.

Other seeds fell into thorny soil. It looked good at first, but then the weeds started to grow at the same time as the plants. The weeds and thorns grew faster and choked the plants so they died as well.

Thankfully, other seeds fell onto good soil. The plants grew well. And the farmer got a healthy crop. There were lots and lots of grain to make many loaves of bread. Jesus then said, 'He who has ears let him hear.'

What does Jesus want you to learn from this story? Some people are like bad soil and some people are like good soil. Some people listen to God and obey him and others don't.

But it is not just people who go to prison who are bad.

If you disobey God in any way you are a sinner.

Some people are like the rocky soil. They might listen to God's Word and even enjoy it a bit, but when troubles come they give up very quickly. They never really loved God at all. If they had they would have kept trusting God even in hard times.

Remember the thorny soil? Sometimes people are just like that. They behave as though they love God, but then they forget about him. They might make a show about listening to God's Word but then other things become more important.

They become worried about other things such as 'Will I have enough food?' or 'Do I have enough money?'

They might think, 'Do I really need to go to church today? I'll do something else instead.'

Thankfully some people are like the good soil. They listen to God's Word, they understand it and they believe it. The good soil produced a good harvest.

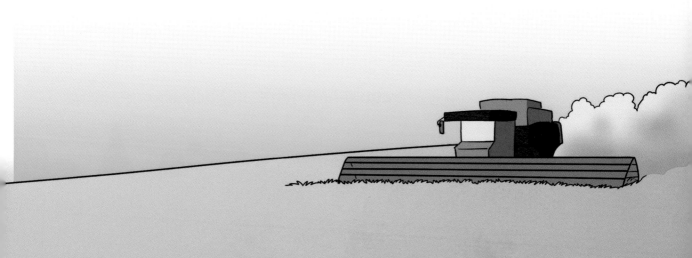

A person who truly loves God produces a good life. They obey God and love him. They love other people and show it by their kind actions.

The plants that grew in the good soil grew well, and they kept growing. Some grew better than others, but they all grew. If you are a person who truly loves God, you will learn about him more and more.

You will grow. Your life will show others what Jesus is like – that he is wonderful.

Christian Focus Publications

Christian Focus Publications publishes books for adults and children under its four main imprints: Christian Focus, CF4K, Mentor and Christian Heritage. Our books reflect our conviction that God's Word is reliable and Jesus is the way to know him, and live for ever with him. Our children's list includes a Sunday School curriculum that covers pre-school to early teens, and puzzle and activity books. We also publish personal and family devotional titles, biographies and inspirational stories that children will love. If you are looking for quality Bible teaching for children then we have an excellent range of Bible stories and age-specific theological books. From pre-school board books to teenage apologetics, we have it covered!

AUTHOR'S DEDICATON: To my friends and family at Kingsview Christian Centre, A.P.C.

10 9 8 7 6 5 4 3 2 1
Copyright © 2017 Catherine Mackenzie
ISBN: 978-1-5271-0093-0
Published in 2017 by Christian Focus Publications Ltd.
Geanies House, Fearn, Tain, Ross-shire, IV20 1TW, Great Britain
Illustrations by Chiara Bertelli
Cover Design: Sarah Korvemaker
Printed in Malta

Scripture quotations are from The Holy Bible, English Standard Version, copyright © 2001 by Crossway Bibles, a division of Good News Publishers. Used by permission. All rights reserved. ESV Text Edition: 2007.